Walt Disney's
DONALD DUCK
ADVENTURES

TAKE-ALONG COMIC

GEMSTONE PUBLISHING
TIMONIUM, MARYLAND

STEPHEN A. GEPPI
*President/Publisher and
Chief Executive Officer*

JOHN K. SNYDER JR.
Chief Administrative Officer

STAFF

LEONARD (JOHN) CLARK
Editor-in-Chief

GARY LEACH
Art Director

SUSAN DAIGLE-LEACH
Production Manager

MELISSA BOWERSOX
Director-Creative Projects

• IN THIS ISSUE •

Donald Duck
THE GHOST RATS OF HAMELIN
Story: Lars Jensen **Art:** Flemming Andersen
Dialogue: Gary Leach

Mickey Mouse
THE TERRIBLE TSUNAMI
Story: Michael T. Gilbert **Art:** Joaquin Cañizares Sanchez

Donald Duck
GHOSTDUSTING...
Story: Rune Meikle **Art:** Miguel Fernandez Martinez
Dialogue: Annette Roman

Original cover and interior color
by **Egmont**
Lettering and color modifications by **Gary Leach**

**ADVERTISING/
MARKETING**

J.C. VAUGHN
Executive Editor
Toll Free
(888) 375-9800 Ext. 413
ads@gemstonepub.com

ARNOLD T. BLUMBERG
Editor

BRENDA BUSICK
Creative Director

JAMIE DAVID
Executive Liaison

SARA ORTT
Assistant Executive Liaison

MARK HUESMAN
Production Assistant

MIKE WILBUR
Shipping Manager

**WALT DISNEY'S
DONALD DUCK
ADVENTURES 6**
Take-Along Comic
May, 2004

Published by
Gemstone Publishing

© 2004 Disney Enterprises, Inc.,
except where noted.
All rights reserved.

Nothing contained herein may be
reproduced without the written
permission of Disney Enterprises,
Inc., Burbank, CA., or other
copyright holders. 12-issue subscription rates: In the U.S.,
$95.40. In Canada, $105.00,
payable in U.S. funds. For advertising rates and information call
(888) 375-9800 ext. 413.
Subscription and advertising
rates subject to change without
notice. Postmaster: send address
changes to Walt Disney's Donald
Duck Adventures / Take-Along
Comic, PO Box 469, West Plains,
MO, 65775.

PRINTED IN CANADA

* SEE DONALD DUCK ADVENTURES #5

WE'VE TOLD YOU *BEFORE*...FREELANCE AGENTS DON'T COME *ASKING* FOR ASSIGNMENTS! *WE* CONTACT *YOU*!

BUT...

AND YOUR SUPERVISOR, AGENT KOLIK, IS GETTING READY FOR ANOTHER ASSIGNMENT! I DON'T LIKE THE IDEA OF YOU HARING OFF *WITHOUT* HER!

BUT I *NEED A BREAK*, HEAD! SOMETHING TO HELP ME OUT FROM UNDER EVERYONE ELSE'S BOOTS!

AND THERE'S THE SMALL MATTER OF *SKIPPING TOWN* BEFORE I'M *LYNCHED*!

THAT'S ENCOURAGING!

ALL RIGHT! I MAY HAVE *SOMETHING*...

I *KNEW* IT!

"EACH YEAR IN HAMELIN, GERMANY, ON THE ANNIVERSARY OF THE PIED PIPER'S LEGENDARY EXTERMINATION JOB, A GANG OF GHOST RATS APPEARS TO MAKE MAYHEM FOR A WEEK! AMATEUR GHOST HUNTERS HAVE TRIED TO TACKLE THEM..."

"...BUT TO NO AVAIL!"

AS THE PROBLEM'S RESTRICTED TO HAMELIN, TNT HASN'T GOTTEN INVOLVED YET! BUT *MAYBE* IT'S TIME WE DID...

OH YES! *ABSOLUTELY!*

DON'T WORRY, HEAD! FETHRY AND I WILL DEAL WITH THIS! NO SWEAT!

OFF WE GO! FIRST, THE ARMORY!

DID YOU NOTICE HOW THE HEAD GAUGED THE PRECISE THREAT LEVEL OF THE GHOST RATS? ONLY A *TRUE EXPERT* ON ARCANE MATTERS COULD...

QUIET, FETHRY!

I'VE READ THAT GHOSTS USE LIGHTS TO LURE MORTALS INTO *TRAPS!*

PHOOEY! WHAT DO GHOST *RATS* KNOW FROM *LIGHTS?*

I'LL COVER YOU WHILE YOU CHECK OUT THE INTERIOR OFFICE!

SO FAR, SO GOOD! FETHRY'S FINALLY LEARNING TO FOLLOW MY LEAD!

THAT'S WHAT *TAKING CHARGE* IS ABOUT - MAKING PEOPLE *SNAP TO!*

HMMM! WONDER WHAT'S *KEEPING* HIM?

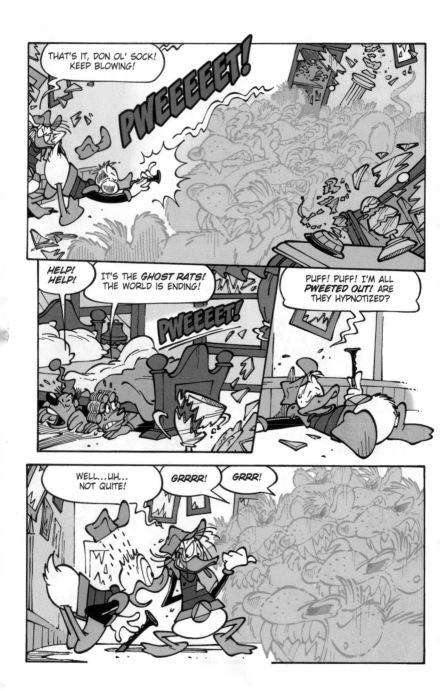

DUCKBURG...

YOUR "GHOST EXTERMINATOR" ROLES *WERE* ONLY *COVERS* FOR YOUR TNT AGENT JOBS! ANY PAYMENT FROM HAMELIN WOULD BE TO TNT, NOT YOU!

HRMPH!

BUT DON'T WORRY, YOU STILL GET YOUR *TNT* PAYCHECKS!

YIPPEE!

MORE GOOD NEWS! SCROOGE MCDUCK JUST RAISED PRICES ON ALL PRODUCTS FROM HIS BAKERIES! EVERYONE'S SO ANGRY AT *HIM* NOW, THEY'VE FORGOTTEN YOUR SKUNK OIL MISHAP!

AND TNT HAS TAKEN CARE OF THE CLEANUP ON *THAT!*

THANKS, HEAD! I REALLY *OWE* YOU ONE!

EXACTLY! IT WAS A MAJOR OPERATION, AND THERE *WERE* CERTAIN *EXPENSES* INVOLVED! YOUR PAYCHECK JUST ABOUT COVERS THEM!

WHAT?!

BUT... BUT...

AND DON'T WORRY ABOUT THE *BALANCE* OF WHAT YOU OWE US!

YOU CAN WORK IT OFF AT THIS *NON-TNT JOB* WE LOCATED FOR YOU! IT HAS TO DO WITH...*KING ARTHUR!*

I...UH...I...

JUNIOR WOODCHUCK MUSEUM · ARTHURIAN COLLECTION

I DON'T GET IT! IF UNCA DONALD WANTED TO WORK HERE, WHY DIDN'T HE JUST ASK *US*?

A NEW JOB WHERE YOU GET TO SHARE YOUR NEPHEWS' INTERESTS! HOW *LUCKY* CAN ONE GUY *BE*?

GRUMBLE!

WALT DISNEY'S MICKEY MOUSE

THE TERRIBLE TSUNAMI

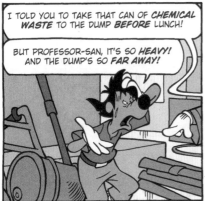

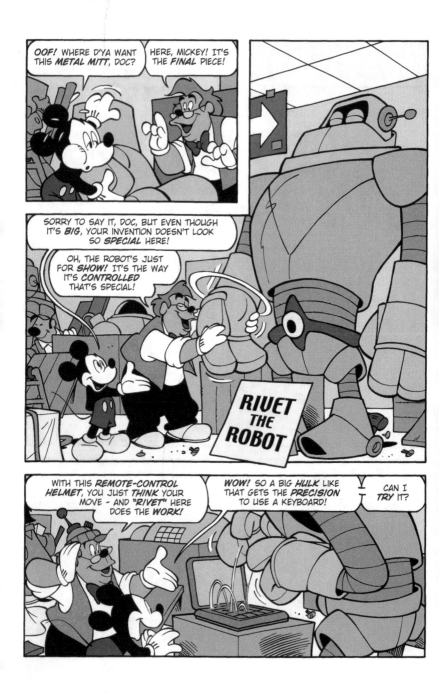

PROFESSOR DHIM SUM! I SHOULD HAVE KNOWN!

DOC STATIC, YOU OLD TEST-TUBE! IT'S GOOD TO SEE YOU AGAIN!

PROFESSOR, I BROUGHT ALONG MY OLD FRIEND MICKEY MOUSE TO HELP ME HERE!

IT IS A GREAT HONOR! STATIC-SAN HAS WRITTEN OF YOU OFTEN!

THAT'S A WATER ROBOT YOU'VE GOT THERE, PROF?

ALMOST, MICKEY! I CALL IT "MOLECULES WITH A MIND"! MY CHEMICAL TREATMENT GIVES THE WATER A SMALL DEGREE OF ARTIFICIAL INTELLIGENCE!

THINKING WATER?

VERY RUDIMENTARY! ONLY ENOUGH TO IMITATE THINGS!

HEY! I KNOW THAT GUY!

AH-CHOO!

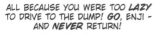

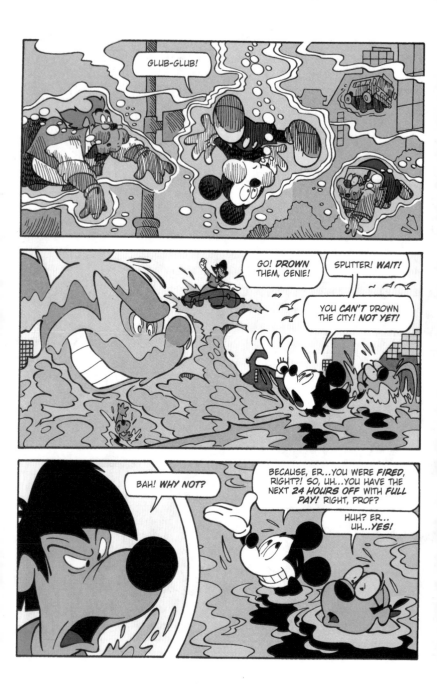

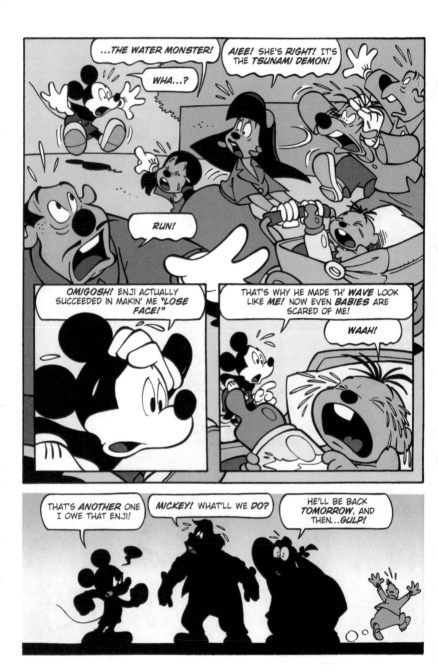

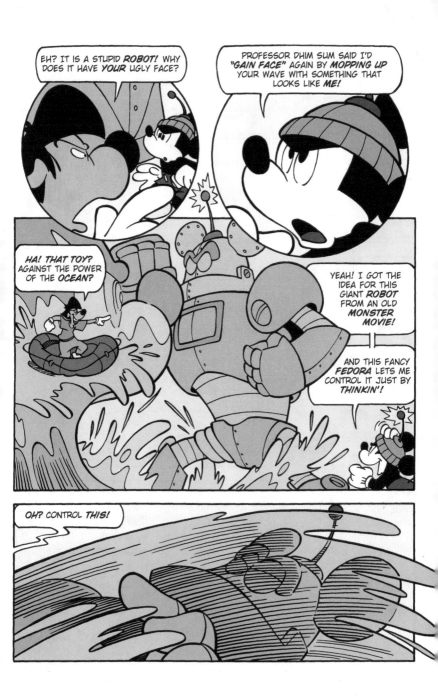

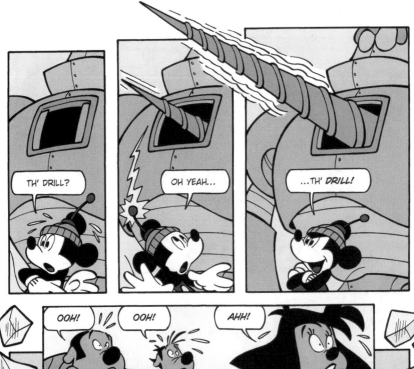

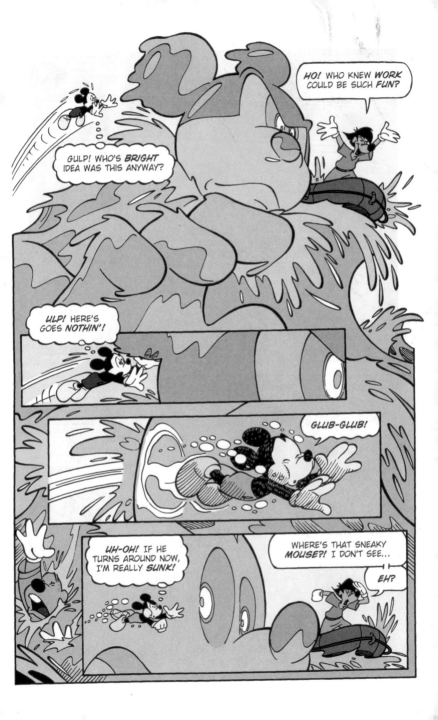

LETTERS

DONALD DUCK ADVENTURES
E-mail: dd@gemstonepub.com
Surface mail: Donald Duck Adventures, 1966 Greenspring Drive Ste. 400,
Timonium MD 21093

Congratulations on another big success...I really enjoyed the new **Donald Duck Adventures** book. It was great having long stories all in one book, rather than chopped up into monthly parts.

"The Deep" was a terrific lead story – I've never seen artwork by Fecchi before, and I thought it was really fresh and fun. The characters all look modern and interesting, especially the nephews, and the detailed backgrounds were great to look at. The big splash panels were just breathtaking. The story was lots of fun, and I liked the twist of the carvings being the monster's comic book art. The whole thing was very clever, and I hope we get to see more from this team.

I also really enjoyed "Panicking Pachyderms" – it was nice to see Mickey in a gentle comedy, rather than his usual detective story. The art was loose and expressive, and very appealing.

"Time of Reckoning" didn't please me quite as much. I usually like science-fiction, but this story had too many far-fetched plot conceits all squished together. Plus, it was just depressing to see Duckburg totally demolished. However, the art was very nice, especially the title page and the "Quack-Fu" computer game pages.

You guys have really surpassed all my expectations for what you would do with the Disney books. I'm really looking forward to seeing what's coming up! Thanks for all your hard work and dedication; I'm sure there are lots of appreciative fans like me.

Danny Horn
via e-mail

We hope so, Danny! We've always tried to provide the best reading experience possible. Of course, it's the readers who will ultimately determine how well we've succeeded!

"The day I see a *real* monster, I'll gladly punch his lights out for you... When I get home, I'll hang up my stockings for Santa! Then, I'll look for leprechauns under the first rainbow!" – Donald Duck, pooh-pooh-er of the paranormal, from **Donald Duck Adventures** 4.

Interesting talk from someone who has closely-encountered the Loup Garou, the Queen of the Wild Dog Pack, Will-O-The-Wisp, Nessie the Loch Ness Monster, a giant jellyfish off the island of Rippan-Taro, a saucer-load of Micro-Ducks from Outer Space, and even "The Thing from Beneath the Oil Rig" from the first issue of this magazine.

It never fails to amuse me when a character expresses surprise, dismay, or staunch skepticism when considering the possibility of any strange or unexplained phenomenon, when said character has seen numerous "other things that go bump in the night" in previous issues or episodes. Oh, well...I suppose it's a necessary storytelling convention to help "ground" our hero(es) into something resembling "our own frame of reference," before sending him, her, or them off on a grand adventure.

Just because it has no letter column (...alas, as is the case with *many* other comic book titles of late), I've neglected to write and tell you that, in my not-so-humble opinion, **Donald Duck Adventures** may very well be the *best* title you publish! And, considering the gobs of praise I've heaped on the other titles of your line in their respective letter columns, this is quite the compliment indeed!

Chock-full of the "meatier" long adventure stories I crave but find all too seldom, even in the best examples of Disney comic books past and present, an issue of **DDA** is a unique reading experience that one can easily lose one's self in for a delightful interlude.

This issue's "Blue Rain," a "James Bond meets Kolchak the Night Stalker meets Men in Black" type of tale, is a prime example of how this material differentiates from the conventional duck fare. Drawn in a looser and more "animated" style than the traditional Barks/Gottfredson/Murry inspired approach that has served these comics well for over 60 years, the visuals are perfectly suited for the stories being told. These are adventures that Donald might share with his Cousin Fethry or Daisy, instead of the usual three nephews, Mickey might share with Minnie, Pluto, or Doc Static, rather than Goofy, and Scrooge even shared with "two versions of his future self" in place of Don and the boys.

Furthermore, the "Take Along Comic" tag certainly lives up its name. I "took along" the first issue of this magazine for my flight back to New York from 2003's San Diego Comic Con International. It lasted me from San Diego to about Washington, DC! Uncle Scrooge would sure be pleased over the "bang" we get for our bucks.

Joe Torcivia
via e-mail

At first, the "Take-Along" format seemed too constricted to do justice to a letter column, but we've now decided to give it a try. We would like to feature them when time and space allow – even when they don't, we are always interested in hearing from you, the readers.

And keep a lookout for our new **Mickey Mouse Adventures** *"Take-Along," coming soon!*

MEET THE NOD SQUAD

Collect bobbleheads, wobblers, or headknockers?

Appearing daily in Scoop!

Daredevil, Jeannie, Spider-Man, the Osbournes, Tony the Tiger, Wonder Woman plus many more of your favorite Yes Men are quaking and quivering through the electronic pages of Scoop. Crammed with earth-shaking character images and the latest industry news, Scoop is the FREE, weekly, e-newsletter from Gemstone Publishing and Diamond International Galleries for collectors and pop culture enthusiasts of all ages. Just visit http://scoop.diamondgalleries.com to check it all out and subscribe. So remember, if you're lacking vital Bobblehead information - don't get the Bobblehead blues, just log onto Scoop for the hottest Bobblehead news!

SCOOP THIS JOINT IS JUMPIN'!

"AND SUPERSTITIOUS FOLK CLAIM TO HEAR EERIE VOICES EMANATING FROM INSIDE ITS WALLS."

"PROBABLY JUST THE WIND HOWLING THROUGH THE RAFTERS."

"BUT WHO'S TO SAY...?"

"MORE IMPORT- ANTLY, TO THE WEST LIES A MAGNIFICENT VIEW OF THE OCEAN! AND THE CLIFF PLUNGES DOWN TO JAGGED ROCKS AND CRASHING SURF!"

"THIS MAJESTIC ABODE STOOD IN SOLITUDE FOR CENTURIES! UNTIL..."

"...HIGHWAY 80 WAS CONSTRUCTED NEARBY! NOW, ONLY A STAND OF TREES SEPARATES IT FROM A BUSY THOROUGHFARE..."

FOR 30 CENTS AN HOUR!?

TWENTY-FOUR HOURS A DAY, SEVEN DAYS A WEEK!

AND OVERTIME?

ALL YOU HAVE TO DO IS *SWEEP* A FEW OLD GHOSTS OUT OF THE ATTIC!

DONALD ISN'T KEEN TO BE A JANITOR...

BUT I'M BROKE!

SIGH...A *SMART, SENSITIVE* DUCK LIKE ME NEEDS A *PROFESSION,* A *CALLING!* NOT A *HOUSECLEANING JOB!*

WELL, LOOKIE HERE...A FLYER FOR A ONE-DAY COURSE IN *"GHOSTDUSTING FOR FUN & PROFIT"*...

HMM! THIS TURN OF EVENTS MIGHT LEAD TO A CAREER MOVE *AFTER ALL!*

HAW! BRING IT ON, *ARMIES OF DARKNESS!* I'LL CHASE YOU PAST *HADES' SUBURBS!*

YEEEK! A G-G-GHOST!

WHAT HAPPENED? ARE YOU ALL RIGHT?

ER...*SURE!* I'M JUST SO *SHOCKINGLY HANDSOME,* IS ALL!

BRR! COLD AND SILENT AS THE GRAVE!

LOOKS AS IF TIME STOOD STILL HERE FOR *CENTURIES!*

COULD BE! THIS PORTRAIT OF *DON DE VILTON* IS FROM THE *SIXTEENTH CENTURY!*

ENOUGH *ART HISTORY,* BOYS! TAKE A GANDER AT *THIS!*

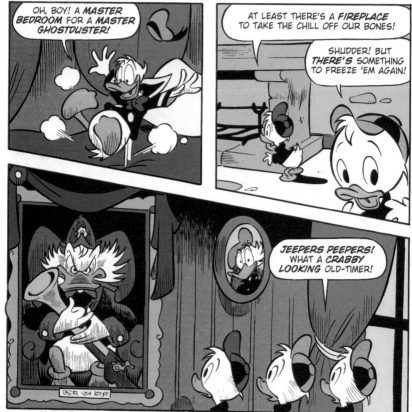

THAT BALEFUL GLEAM IN HIS EYES SENDS ICY SHIVERS DOWN MY BACKBONE!

SAYS HERE HE'S *COLONEL DANJERUSDUCK DEVILTON*—THE *LAST DESCENDANT* OF THE DEVILTON CLAN!

THE PORTRAIT'S SO *LIFELIKE!* IT'S LIKE HE'S LOOKING *RIGHT AT US!*

I HOPE *HE* ISN'T THE GHOST WHO'S HAUNTING THIS JOINT! UNCA DONALD WOULD BE NO MATCH FOR *HIM!*

YEP! HE'D BE DOOMED!

A DAY AGO, MAYBE, BUT WITH MY *PH.D. IN GHOSTDUSTING* AND THIS *GHOSTDUSTING KIT,* IT'LL BE A *PIECE OF DEVIL'S FOOD CAKE!*

THIS IS THE *DELUXE* OUTFIT, SPECIAL ORDERED FROM *PROFESSOR BLABBERBUNK!*

NEVER HEARD OF THE GUY!

ISN'T IT A LITTLE *LATE* FOR *HALLOWEEN,* UNCA DONALD?

TUT, *NAIVE YOUTH!*

AH! *GHOSTDUSTING FOR GENIUSES,* BY PROFESSOR BLABBERBUNK! *THE COMPLETE GUIDE TO THAT WHICH GOES BUMP IN THE NIGHT!*

TEXTBOOKS SCARE *STUDENTS,* NOT *EVIL SPIRITS,* UNCA DONALD.

DOUBTING DEWEY! HOW *DARE* YOU QUESTION PROFESSOR BLABBERBUNK'S WISDOM AND EDJUMACATION!

THE BOYS WISELY DECIDE THIS IS AS GOOD A TIME AS ANY TO GATHER FIREWOOD...

THE GROUNDS ARE AS DARK AND GLOOMY AS A *HORROR MOVIE LOCATION!*

STOP! YOU'RE GIVING ME THE *CREEPS!*

LOOKS *ANCIENT* — MUCH OLDER THAN THE *MANSION!*

ANYBODY HOME?

SHUDDER! IT'S A *MAUSOLEUM!*

WONDER *WHO'S* LAID TO REST HERE?

Within these walls sleeps the brave captain of the Duckalusian Armada, Don de Vilton. As well as his devoted sons, who built the Devilton Mansion and carry on his noble duty!

GEE!

I'D GIVE *TWO POUNDS OF WOODCHUCK MEDALS* TO FIND OUT WHAT THIS MYSTERIOUS DEVILTON FAMILY'S "DUTY" IS!

LOOK! THE **TOMB** OF THAT CREEPY GUY IN THE **PAINTING!**

COLONEL DANJERUSDUCK

I DON'T KNOW ABOUT **YOU,** BUT I COULD USE SOME FRESH AIR ABOUT NOW!

DITTO!

FORTUN-ATELY, A WARM, CRACKLING FIRE SOON DISPELS THE CHILL MOOD.

LISTEN AND LEARN, INFANTS! THE **FLABBERGASTING WISDOM** OF PROFESSOR BLABBERBUNK...

"TO **IMMUNIZE** THYSELF AGAINST EVIL GNOMES, GOBLINS, GHOSTS, AND TOOTH FAIRIES, THOU MUST RUB THYSELF IN A **SACRED OINTMENT** OF **MOLDY CHEESE,** GARLIC, AND **SMOKED HERRING!"**

"THEREAFTER, THOU MUST CHANT **"FLOPPYTIBUS BOBBYTIMUS"** 200 TIMES WHILE THOU DOST STAND ON THINE HEAD WITH THINE LEFT BIG TOE IN THINE RIGHT EAR!"

DON'T THOU THINKEST IT'S TIME TO SEE WHAT THE *JUNIOR WOODCHUCK'S GUIDEBOOK* HATH TO SAY ABOUT THE PROFESSOR'S ODORIFEROUS OINTMENTS?!

SNORT!

PHOOEY ON YOUR *KNOW-IT-ALL* GUIDEBOOK! I'LL PUT *MY MONEY* ON PROFESSOR BLABBERBUNK ANYTIME!

IF ANY *BOGEYMEN* DARE TO SHOW THEIR *BOGEYMUGS* TONIGHT, THEY'RE ASKING FOR TROUBLE!

YAWN!

SEEMS OUR BOGEYMAN IS *ALREADY* SHOWING HIS MUG! WHAT'S THIS COLONEL DANJER-USDUCK'S STORY, ANYWAY?

IT SAYS ON THE BRASS PLATE THAT HE WAS "LOYAL TO THE CAUSE IN LIFE *AND DEATH*"!

BRR! THAT'S ENOUGH! LET'S *PULL THE COVERS OVER OUR HEADS* AND *TRY TO SLEEP!*

IS IT A TRICK OF THE LIGHT...? OR DO THE BALEFUL EYES OF THE PORTRAIT FOLLOW THE DUCKLINGS TO THEIR REPOSE?!

IT'S JUST SOME KIND OF MECHANICAL TOMB-OPENER...I *H-HOPE!*

N-NO NEED TO GET *SPOOKED!*

WE'VE *SEEN* SKELETONS...

HUH?!

IT'S *EMPTY!*

SO WHAT HAPPENED TO COLONEL DANJERUSDUCK'S EARTHLY REMAINS? THE MYSTERY *DEEPENS...*

SNIFF! THAT *SMELL...*

THE MANSION'S *ON FIRE!*

THE SMOKE'S COMING FROM *OUR BEDROOM!*

FORTUNATELY, IT'S A FALSE ALARM...

URGH! PUT ME ASHORE, I'M *SICK* OF THIS *SKUNK CRUISE!*

YUK! THIS "HIGH-TECH INCENSE" IS *HIGH-STINK TROUBLE!*

WONDER IF *THIS* EVER HAPPENED TO THE GOOD PROFESSOR?

TOOT! TOOT!

COUGH! THAT GHOST ALMOST GOT ME!

FINE! IF IT'S *WAR* YOU WANT THEN IT'S *WAR* YOU'LL GET!

SNAP!

#@!★

CRUNCH!

YEEOOW!

LOOK! THERE'S A *HOLE* BEHIND THE PAINTING...

...AND IT'S FILLED WITH *OLD BOOKS!*

THAT CREEPY PORTRAIT WAS *GUARDING* THIS *HIDING PLACE!*

WE'RE IN LUCK! THESE ARE THE DEVILTON'S *DIARIES!*

THIS ONE BELONGED TO DON DE VILTON...AND IT DATES BACK ALL THE WAY TO OCTOBER OF *1589!*

THAT'S THE GUY IN THE PAINTING IN THE HALL!

LISTEN TO THIS...

"OCTOBER THE 16TH, 1589. I, DON DE VILTON, CAPTAIN OF THE DUCKALUSIAN ARMADA AND KNIGHT OF THE CROSS, COMMIT THESE SAD LINES TO THE PAGE IN A STATE OF PROFOUND DESPAIR AND PERPLEXITY."

"A TERRIBLE STORM HAS RAVAGED THESE CURSED WATERS FOR WEEK UPON WEEK."

"HIS MAJESTY, THE DUCKALUSIAN EMPEROR, HAS ENTRUSTED ME TO TRANSPORT THE SPOILS OF WAR TO OUR NATION."

"BUT THE CREW TIRES OF THESE BEDEVILED WATERS, AND I SENSE A MUTINY IS BREWING."

"OCTOBER THE 25TH. THE GALE HATH BLOWN MY VESSEL TOWARD A FOREIGN COAST AND ENEMY WARSHIPS HAVE SPOTTED US."

"I FEAR OUR TREASURE IS NO LONGER SAFE ABOARD OUR VESSEL."

"OCTOBER THE 27TH. ON THE PRETEXT OF PROCURING EXOTIC SPICES, I SET OUT FOR THE COAST ALONE..."

"...WELL AWARE THAT THIS MIGHT BE JUST THE OPPORTUNITY MY CREW AWAITED TO RID THEMSELVES OF ME."

"I HARDLY REACHED THE SHORE WHEN THOSE COWARDLY SEADOGS SET SAIL FOR THE OPEN OCEAN."

"NATURALLY, THEY WERE UNAWARE THAT I HAD UNBURDENED THE SHIP OF THE CONTENTS OF ITS LARDER..."

...AS WELL AS THE CHEST WHICH – BELIEVED TO BE FULL OF HEDGE CLIPPERS – IN FACT CONTAINED THE TREASURE OF THE ARMADA!"

"OCTOBER THE 28TH. THE GODDESS OF FORTUNE HAS SMILED UPON ME. I HAVE CHANCED UPON A LARGE GROTTO NEARBY."

"AS I AM IN UNCHARTED TERRITORY, I MUST TAKE EVERY PRECAUTION TO GUARD HIS MAJESTY'S TREASURE..."

"...AND THIS IS THE PERFECT HIDING PLACE!"

"TO MY SURPRISE, WHEN I REACHED THE BOTTOM OF THE GROTTO, I FOUND ANOTHER CAVERN."

"EVENTUALLY, I FOUND AN EGRESS ONTO THE TOP OF THE CLIFF. THIS HAS GIVEN ME AN IDEA..."

"OCTOBER THE 30TH. TODAY I BLOCKED OFF THE OCEAN ENTRANCE TO THE GROTTO, LEAVING JUST ONE PATH TO THE TREASURE..."

"AND THE ENTRANCE IS EASY TO GUARD SINGLE-HANDEDLY UNTIL THE EMPEROR SENDS REINFORCEMENTS."

"JANUARY THE 10TH, 1590. I HAVE BUILT A HUMBLE STONE ABODE WITH MY BARE HANDS AND BY THE SWEAT OF MY BROW ATOP THE ENTRANCE TO THE GROTTO.

"MARCH THE 5TH, 1591. STILL NO SIGN OF REIN-FORCEMENTS."

"NEWS OF THE TREASURE'S DISAPPEARANCE SHOULD HAVE REACHED THE EMPEROR BY NOW. BUT I AM POSSESSED OF GREAT PATIENCE..."

"DECEMBER THE 14TH, 1625. WEEKS HAVE TURNED TO MONTHS, AND MONTHS TO YEARS...I AM AN OLD MAN NOW, MARRIED TO A FINE LOCAL WOMAN AND BLESSED WITH A STRONG SON TO CARRY ON THE PROUD LINEAGE AND DUTY OF THE DE VILTONS."

"HE SHALL LEARN THE SECRET OF HIS MAJESTY'S TREASURE, AND GUARD IT HIMSELF WHEN THE TIME COMES." THAT'S THE END OF THE DIARY!

WOW!

THE WOODCHUCK'S GUIDEBOOK SAYS THE EMPEROR WAS *OVERTHROWN* IN THE DUCKALLUSIAN REVOLUTION...

...IN *OCTOBER OF 1589*, WHILE THE ARMADA WAS *LOST AT SEA!*

NO *WONDER* A RESCUE PARTY NEVER SHOWED UP!

BUT WHAT ABOUT THE TREASURE?

MAYBE *DANJERUSDUCK DEVILTON'S* JOURNAL WILL TELL US...

"IN THIS YEAR OF GRACE 1869, I, COLONEL DANJERUSDUCK, EX-COMMANDER OF THE GOOSEBURY FUSILIERS AND THE LAST DESCENDANT OF THE DEVILTONS (FORMERLY DE VILTONS)..."

"...CONCLUDE OUR FAMILY HISTORY WITH THE FOLLOWING FACTS OF MY OWN LIFE."

"I LIVE ALONE IN THE HOUSE BUILT BY MY VENERABLE FOREFATHERS."

"HERE I HAVE VIGILANTLY GUARDED THE EMPEROR'S TREASURE."

"INEXPLICABLY, NOT ONE OF THE LOCAL GENTS HAS OFFERED ME THE HAND OF HIS DAUGHTER IN MARRIAGE."

"THUS I HAVE NO HEIR TO WHOM I CAN PASS ON OUR FAMILY'S SACRED DUTY."

"AND SO I HAVE TAKEN EXTRAORDINARY PRECAUTIONS TO PROTECT THE TREASURE AFTER MY DEMISE."

"THOUGH FORGETFULNESS CREEPS UPON ME WITH THE WANING YEARS, THIS I SHALL NEVER FORGET..."

"...TO GUARD THE TREASURE, ONCE ENTRUSTED TO MY ANCESTOR DON DE VILTON, WITH MY *LIFE!*"

WHAT A STORY! SO *THAT'S* WHY DANJERUSDUCK HAUNTS THIS HOUSE! HE'S *STILL* GUARDING THE TREASURE!

EVEN *AFTER* HE DIED!

SO THE TREASURE MUST STILL BE IN A GROTTO UNDER THIS HOUSE!

STOP *TREMBLING* SO I CAN MAKE A *NICE, BIG HOLE* IN YOU!

BLABBERBUNK DIDN'T SAY ANYTHING ABOUT *ARMED* GHOSTS!

BOOM!

CONFOUND IT! MUST BE *MICE* IN THE BARREL AGAIN!

LUCKY YOU, UNCA DONALD!

THE SHOTGUN AND BULLETS AREN'T ANY MORE SOLID THAN THE GHOST! THEY CAN'T HURT US!

THEN PRICK UP YOUR TRANSPARENT EARS AND SWOON TO PROFESSOR BLABBERBUNK'S *DISAPPARATING INCANTATION!*

?

FIDDLE-DEE-DEE! FEE FI FO FUM...

AGH! YOUR CHANTING'S WORSE THAN THAT *NEW-FANGLED ROCK N' ROLL!*

WHAT'S HE UP TO *NOW?*

ZOINK!

UH-OH! HE SUDDENLY DOESN'T LOOK *TRANS-LUCENT* ANYMORE!

BIPPITY BOPPITY...

...BOO!?

THIS CAN'T BE HAPPENING! THE GHOST IS *KIDNAPPING* UNCA DONALD!

OCTOPUS, RHINOCEROS, HIPPOPOTA-MUS...

OUTNUMBERED! I HAD BEST WITHDRAW TO THE TURRET WITH MY CAPTIVE!

WHAT ARE WE GONNA DO? HOW COULD THIS HAPPEN?

I DON'T GET IT! THE JUNIOR WOODCHUCK'S GUIDEBOOK SAYS GHOSTS ARE *HARMLESS*...

UH-OH! I FORGOT TO CHECK THE *FOOTNOTES!* TURNS OUT CERTAIN GHOSTS CAN *GAIN* SOLID FORM...

...IF THEIR *WILLPOWER* IS STRONG ENOUGH!

BUT THEY NEED TO *CONCENTRATE* MIGHTY HARD TO STAY SOLID...

COME ON!

I FOUND UNCA DONALD'S BOOK! THE TRAIL LEADS TO THIS *OPEN WINDOW!*

CAN THE SARCASM! WE JUST SAW *INDISPUTABLE PROOF* OF THIS BOOK'S *EFFECTIVENESS!*

GHOST-DUSTING FOR GENIUSES

YOU CAN'T DENY I'D NEVER HAVE WON OUR FIRST BATTLE WITHOUT IT!

GHOST-DUSTING FOR

BUT THAT'S JUST THE *BEGINNING!* UNTIL THIS PLACE IS *PHANTASM FREE,* YOU KIDS BETTER RUN OUT AND PLAY IN THE SUNSHINE!

WHAT SUNSHINE?

LOOKS LIKE WE'LL HAVE TO SOLVE THIS CASE OURSELVES, MEN!

SO WHAT ELSE IS NEW?!

DON DE VILTON WROTE THAT HE BUILT HIS HOUSE ON THE ENTRANCE TO THE GROTTO, RIGHT?

YEAH...BUT WHAT *PART* OF THE HOUSE?

OUR GHOST PAL KNEW WHERE IT WAS...

BUT WE CAN'T FIND ANY SIGNS OF A SECRET DOOR OR FALSE FLOOR!

WAIT A MINUTE! THAT *STRANGE FIREPLACE...!*

I BET THIS WAS DE VIL- TON'S *ORIGINAL* COTTAGE! ONCE THEY BUILT THE MAN- SION, THIS BECAME THE *FAMILY MAUSOLEUM!*

SO THIS ISN'T FOR KEEPING GHOSTS' TOOTSIES TOASTY?

BINGO, GUYS!

LOOK WHAT I FOUND!

COLON

A TRAPDOOR UNDER A LOOSE SLAB AT THE BOTTOM OF THE TOMB!

BUILDING HIS *OWN TOMB* ON TOP OF THE ENTRANCE...SOUNDS LIKE AN *"EXTRAORDINARY PRECAUTION,"* ALL RIGHT!

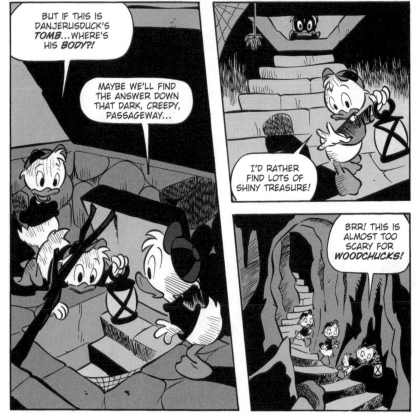

BUT IF THIS IS DANJERUSDUCK'S *TOMB*...WHERE'S HIS *BODY?!*

MAYBE WE'LL FIND THE ANSWER DOWN THAT DARK, CREEPY, PASSAGEWAY...

I'D RATHER FIND LOTS OF SHINY TREASURE!

BRR! THIS IS ALMOST TOO SCARY FOR *WOODCHUCKS!*

MEANWHILE, DONALD HAS BEGUN "PLAN B"...

IN INSTANCES OF PARTICULARLY *STUBBORN* GHOSTS, PROFESSOR BLABBERBUNK RECOMMENDS *EXPLOSIVE MEASURES*...

"SIMPLY STRIKE AT ITS FAVORITE *HAUNTING GROUND*"!

THE PROFESSOR'S WISDOM IS TRULY *PARANORMAL!*

THIS GHOSTDUSTING KIT EVEN COMES WITH A KEG OF *DISAPPARATING POWDER!*

GUARANTEED NOT TO DAMAGE THE PREMISES, EXCEPT FOR A LITTLE *SOOT*...

BUT IT'LL CREATE A *PSYCHIC BLAST* ON THE *PLASMA-GORICAL LEVEL*... AND A LOT OF *NEAT SMOKE!*

HELLO, NEPHEW!

WHY, UNCLE SCROOGE! WHAT BRINGS *YOU* HERE?

THOUGHT I'D POP BY TO INSPECT YOUR PROGRESS.

HEY! NO *COSTUME PARTIES* TILL THE HOTEL OPENS!

THIS IS MY *GHOSTDUSTING* UNIFORM! I DRESS FOR SUCCESS!

IN FACT, YOU'VE ARRIVED JUST IN TIME TO WITNESS THE *PERMANENT EXTERMINATION* OF YOUR *GHOST VERMIN* WITH MY *SPECIAL BOMB!*

A *BOMB!* IN MY *MULTIMILLION-DOLLAR HOTEL?*

HAVE NO FEAR!

IT'S *ABSOLUTELY HARMLESS!* A *FAINT "POP"* AND A *BIT OF SMOKE* – THAT'S ALL!

HARRUMPH!

THAT'S WHAT I HIRED YOU FOR, I GUESS! BUT IF YOU DAMAGE SO MUCH AS A FLOORBOARD...

UNCA DONALD... AND UNCA SCROOGE!

GUESS WHAT *WE* FOUND!?

A CHEST LOADED WITH THE *LOST TREASURE* OF THE DUCKALUSIAN ARMADA!

THE LOST DUCKALUSIAN TREASURE?

YEAH! IT'S HIDDEN IN A SECRET GROTTO RIGHT UNDER THE MANSION'S MASTER BEDROOM! IT'S *FULL* OF *GOLD AND JEWELS!*

AND YOU SHOULD SEE HOW WELL IT'S *PROTECTED!* THE *WHOLE GROTTO* IS *CRAMMED* WITH *EXPLOSIVES!*

Y-YOU DON'T SAY...

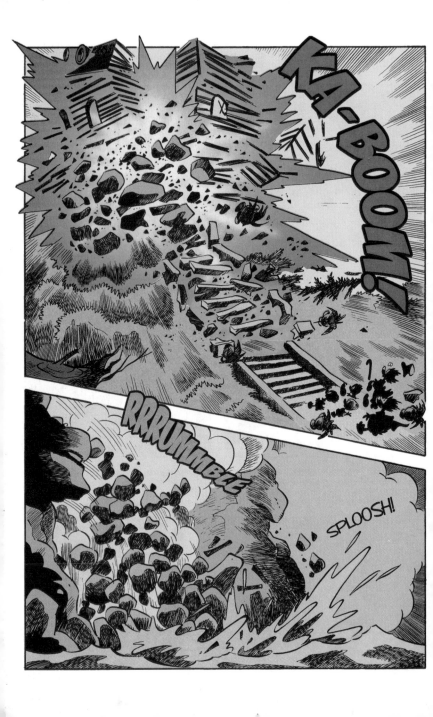

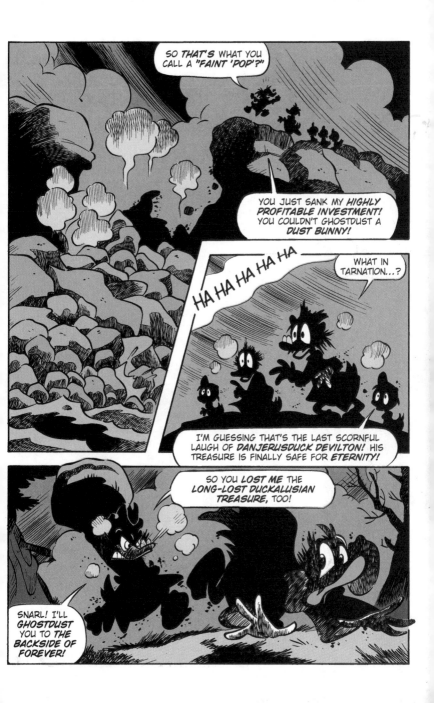

3 1524 00452 0138